Gentle Grasp

Gentle Grasp

Poems
by

Laura Daniels

© 2024 Laura Daniels. All rights reserved.
This material may not be reproduced in any form, published,
reprinted, recorded, performed, broadcast,
rewritten or redistributed without
the explicit permission of Laura Daniels.
All such actions are strictly prohibited by law.

Cover design by Shay Culligan
Cover image by azndc, an istock image from Getty Images
Author photo by Laura Daniels

ISBN: 978-1-63980-663-8

Kelsay Books
502 South 1040 East, A-119
American Fork, Utah 84003
Kelsaybooks.com

Chris, Jon, & Deb
three shining stars in my orbit

Acknowledgments

With appreciation to the following publications that published these poems, sometimes in earlier versions:

Annual National Poetry Month Celebration Anthology April 2023: "Any Other Name: A Sonnet"

Goldfinch 25th Edition: "In the Morning"

Journal of New Jersey Poets: "JOY: A Golden Shovel," "Reflection: A Golden Shovel"

New Jersey Bards Poetry Review: "Sunday Cooking" (2022), "Bay Swimming" (2023), "Bluebird Sky" (2024)

Panoply, a Literary Zine, Issue 26: "Mighty Oak: A Haibun"

Platform Review: "Life Lessons"

Poetry for Mental Health: "Wabi Sabi"

Silver Birch's "All About My Mother" Series: "Brewed Rite"

Silver Birch's "Spices & Seasonings" Series: "Frosted Winter Day"

The Writers Club: "Honey"

U.S.1 Worksheets: "Smells Like Jersey Shore"

Visible Ink Anthology 2023/2024: "Double Crossed"

Contents

Courting the Count	13
Bay Swimming	15
Sunday Cooking	16
Party of One	17
Life Lessons	18
Broken	19
Come Out of the Shadow	20
Honey	22
Anna/An Inventory	23
Deep Listening	24
Double Crossed	26
Centering	27
Tradition	29
The End Is Hard to Write	31
Me and My Jonny Dee	32
Silence Speaks Volumes	33
Frosted Winter Day	34
Songs Finally Sung	35
The End Game	37
Breaking Dawn	38
Brewed Rite	39
The Unseatable Bench	40
Mighty Oak: A Haibun	41
Reflection: A Golden Shovel	42
poem at sixty	43
This Being Human	44
swimming	45
Any Other Name: A Sonnet	46
In the Morning	47
Oscar	48
Creating Kintsugi	49
Wabi Sabi	50

Fire Within	51
Bluebird Sky	52
Gentle Grasp	53
JOY: A Golden Shovel	54
Fireflies and Marshmallows	55
Magic Fabric	56
Smells Like Jersey Shore	57
Somersaults with Graceful Flips: A Golden Shovel	59

Courting the Count

It ends a second before you're ready
please stay to watch the credits

fragile second
creation second
birth second
child second
future second

Born into a second bubble
one beat exploding into the next

adult second
drunk second
dangerous second
carefree second

Each snowflake second floating
down till it's lost on the ground

argument second
agreement second
forgiving second

A run-on second
no chance to catch its breath

heavy second
fading second

Fighting to corral
to herd a second

too soon, not yet

you're unable to slow
the stampeding

last second

Bay Swimming

If I ventured in, canvas sneakers remained on
sockless feet, protection from the murky brackish
greenish water with no bottom. White undershirt
stayed on over bathing suit, protection from
the blazing Jersey sun at a time before sunblock.

Haltingly, I chanced going deeper
wet sneakers hindered rapid movements.
Arms above head swung Frankenstein-style
trying not to get my top half wet, not an easy feat
but doable, if no one splashed.

Cousins were fast to the floating pontoon
unencumbered by sneakers and shirts.
From there, they dove, played tag
performed underwater back flips and belly flops.
Even my sister joined in. I did not.

Not knowing this 1970s bay water was polluted,
the beach was open to swimming and fishing.
It was our summer spot, our Jersey Riviera.

Being the youngest, I did not get to the floating raft
often, instead, I spent my time in the shallows, asking:
When are you coming back to the beach?

Sunday Cooking

Slept through electric can opener buzzing
like an alarm clock blaring before sunrise

when the whizzing finally stopped
clanging banging pots and pans reverberated
through the air, which meant a search
for the right-sized saucepan and fryer had begun

finally roused from bed by the beckoning smell
of olive oil that sizzled and browned baseball
sized meatballs of blended beef and pork

once done, they rested on brown paper, stained
with excess released grease, had one
for breakfast with Mom's blessing

the sauce began a soft rolling boil
unleashing a fragrance of tangy tomato
as it started its long journey to perfection

an hour before dinner, meatballs married sauce
just enough time to blend flavors and build up
anticipation for the big meal at three.

Party of One

Eleven years old
in bed knowing
there's whiskey
in the pantry
across the hall

Ma's distracted
by Ed Sullivan

I scoot out
sneak swigs
hidden behind
a cabinet door
no ginger ale
straight, not bad
tastes like more

Dizzy
head wobbly
feet shaky
stumbling to the toilet

I'm gonna blow
liquid regurgitation
empties bottle
into barf

Sweaty relief
television booms
me back to bed
party's over

Life Lessons

Bayway Avenue separated
me from ninth grade
Roosevelt Middle School
and the Bayway Diner

After school, I changed
in the diner bathroom
abracadabra, my gold polyester
uniform morphed me into a waitress

Truck drivers from the NJ Turnpike
idled their trucks in the parking lot
sitting for hours, drinking coffee
making small talk

Midwestern truckers tipped best
Southern truckers smoothly said:
this (lousy) *quarter is for you*
I smiled and kept pouring

Schoolwork got done
and the money earned bought
a half-share in my sister's car
I was too young to drive

Broken

It was all fun and games, experimenting with psychedelics
Opening doors closed for my protection

My hinge broke, damaged pieces came belching out
Thoughts beyond reality, what's real, what's delusional?

My hurt ached, despair so deep, sorrow so sad
Make it stop, help me cope, I was empty of all hope

It was not easy fixing disfigured thoughts
Drugs numb, hide, but don't heal the mutilation

Put back together like a precious porcelain bowl
Not able to see the Kintsugi created

Shamed instead by the breakage, never knowing if
this was preventable, guilt festered like a poisoned stew

Lying awake each night anxious and worried if
my undercover cracks were still visible

I concealed them, mortified my inner demons
might escape, ever fearful of revealing too much

Help finally arrived through therapeutic wisdom
Wounds were remedied by healing salve

A name was given to the abnormality
A title I embraced like a bejeweled brooch

Hello, My Name is Depression

The term sounded so mild, living with it, so debilitating
but finding out opened the door to my salvation

Come Out of the Shadow

blonde green-eyed curious laughter
happiness evaporated overnight
transformed light into darkness
Cimmerian garden flora
unable to root, nothing
grew in shadow

unknown
unwanted
unwelcomed

understanding sought
understanding withered

hidden orb without an orbit
institutionalized, mistreated, abused

coveted domiciled sanctuary, solace
not an unhealthy, harmful sanitarium

escaped, eluded—captured, confused
unrelenting rhythm unsustained

blonde green-eyed scrutinized scowl
aged fast, not cured as intended
released unrooted
time prescribed
to transform
darkness to light

flourished in illumination
finally got grounding
began to bloom

known
wanted
welcomed

roots spread
roots deepened

Honey

a sweet-sounding name
for a vile person

born in 1912
never married

she lived in a railroad apartment
with her roommate Helen
a woman whom she met at work

her two favorite pastimes:
playing pinochle and
making racist judgments

in that way, she didn't discriminate
she thought all were beneath her

each Sunday, she stood with her xenophobic mouth
wide open, the same mouth that spewed hatred
all week, now ready to receive the holiest
of sacraments, how pious she was on that one day

she was the family matriarch
a black mark on my ancestral history

a lineage skeleton
hidden but not forgotten

I feared speaking up, for that
I ask forgiveness and repent

exposing her shameful behavior
is my first step toward reconciliation

Anna/An Inventory

after Lauren Russell's "Peggy/An Inventory"

She wears earplugs and plays a white noise machine to diffuse and quiet the air so she can better hear the thoughts stirring behind her pondering eyes. She has long blunt hair and a curvy figure, both developed and nurtured. She keeps her fingernails short and her toenails polished because that's the perk provided by the shop where they're trimmed. She uses her own expressive words: "re visioning" for edits, "chello" for cheery hello, and "co inside dance" for coincidence. She's not a busybody when she looks out the window; she's neighborhood-watching. She loves the sound wine makes when it's first poured—glug, glug, glug—because happy sounds should be amplified. She finger waves to little ones who make eye contact on her daily morning walk around Warren Street. She watches for the Wren to sing in the warming weather. She wonders if it's the same Wren returning each spring. She ruminates on whether it might be his son or brother or best friend. He (she knows it's a male) looks and sounds the same each year. She speaks low from the belly to get attention. She speaks childlike to shine and lighten the air. She picks up her pen to heal write. She makes sense of her world through words. She writes to let out all that is contained but churning to be released.

Deep Listening

I asked my advisor for guidance on a message
received from a friend who denigrated
a medical treatment my sister received.

      *

She counseled:
*When a person writes such a strong statement,
it's their fear talking. They want to help
but don't realize how their communication
lands when it's read.*

*I don't think it's meant to be mean-spirited.
Can you pray for understanding?*

      *

I breathed my reply:
I will try.

      *

And so began my litany:
*I pray for the soulful guidance needed to
unravel this message with a kind heart.*

*I pray for the strength to rein in judgment
to understand not only the words but
their deeper meaning and reason for being.*

*I seek to discern the distress behind this discord
which was designed to help and not hurt.*

I pray for the sentience to bring forth compassionate forgiveness and fellowship for the correspondent.

With your guiding spirit, may it be so.

Double Crossed

Dear Cee,

We peacefully partnered for over fifty years. You grew as I grew. Both of us changed as we aged, becoming denser and more substantial as we progressed from child to adult, and then from motherhood to menopause.

Back when we were in our thirties, we learned the customary dance. You knew your steps, and I knew mine. We did this repetitive do-si-do as the technician scanned the images on the screen. At the end of the perennial boogie-woogie, we'd hear: *All clear, see you next year.*

But not this time, this time, you lost your footing, and your imperfections sashayed onto the dance floor. Our shared rhythm was destroyed, ruined in an instant. Our graceful duet ended that day. We would never "trip the light fantastic" again. I wanted you removed right from my sight, and I wanted you to take your left friend with you.

I want you to know that you changed me that day from a prancing dancer to a patient with cancer. But I also became a thriving survivor despite your efforts. Yes, I look different, but I'm also freer, lighter, healthier. Your betrayal will never be forgotten or forgiven.

Good riddance,

Your Human Vessel

Centering

to absorb
those hard
tough bits
before
it's too late

laughing mouth
not touching
mourning eyes
loving you
at the end

is hard
I want to
look away
ignore
what's coming

we grasp
we grieve
we gaze
at the sunset

no bickering
no judgment
no solutions

just listening
accepting
being

wanting to say
everything
before it's
too late

here's hoping
heaven's
a lot
like
love

Tradition

We hosted our first Thanksgiving
a holiday about gathering and getting together
in our one-bedroom, third-floor walkup

emptied our living quarters
moved furniture to the attic
brought in a rented folding table

it was a hit

after dinner
Dad slept on the couch
guys watched football
gals washed dishes
kids played on the floor

a new family tradition began

years rolled by, the family expanded
we hosted dinner in West Orange
until we moved to a home in Verona

each year bigger, better than the last
until elders died, youngsters matured
and a new norm was needed

let's go to a restaurant
let's modernize tradition

but it wasn't the same
no leftovers, no mixing
no mingling, no chatting
no snacking after everyone left

no lasting pleasure
in having the family together
only quick goodbyes in a dark
restaurant parking lot

The End Is Hard to Write

Last year marked your first
emergency hospital trip.
This year scored another medical crisis.

I found you on an ER gurney, unconscious
hooked up to an external pacemaker, organs failing.
The doctor said: *If she makes it through
the night, a permanent pacemaker will be inserted
in the morning.*

The next day, you were alert, responding
like your old self but with a new pacemaker.

But I knew, I could feel
we were coming to an end.

Each time, instead of happiness
my heart hurt. I already
mourned you.

Each moment celebrated—
Halloween, Thanksgiving
Christmas, New Year's Eve
Easter, Birthdays
—in mourning's shadow.

Then Mother's Day—
I picked you up, we went to breakfast
lingered over tea, conversation slowed
as your energy drained. I returned you home.
Guided you to bed. Monday
you died—the mourning now immortal.

Me and My Jonny Dee

you altered my essence the moment
you journeyed into existence, nine
pounds of roly-poly loving vibrations

when you first cried
I panicked and called the doctor:
why is my happy baby crying?
the doctor replied:
he's hungry. feed him more

problem solved, you returned to being my baby joy
my chubby chicken, always down for a ride along

I remember our first night at the diner
just me and my Jonny Dee—

you in your baby seat, nibbling a crust of bread
wiggling your toes while I savored supper
with my blossoming baby buddy

Silence Speaks Volumes

after a long day of laundry and cooking
the baby monitor finally falls silent
pressure I didn't know I was holding, releases
peace descends over the house like a cozy
cashmere quilt, muting the television noise
I unwind into the surround sound of silence
eyes unplug, shoulders descend, breath expands

Frosted Winter Day

We wake to fresh winter snow
hear that school is canceled

Kids dress to sled and shovel
I begin thinking about lunch

I take out frozen leftovers saved
from last week's roasted chicken

I search for Mom's yellow
Le Creuset Dutch Oven
stored in the pantry cabinet

I fill it with fresh water
settle in stripped bones
heat to a roaring boil
to bring forth the broth

Once done
stock is strained
meat added, while
I slowly slice in celery
onions and carrots

Today's soup includes parsley
lemongrass and rosemary
a pinch of salt invites in
briny flavor

My restorative savory chicken veggie soup
(one of the few I can make from scratch)
thaws us on this frosted winter day

Songs Finally Sung

I

Your death
delivered
grief filled
black thorned roses.

II

She dammed up
whispered lyrics.
Shadowed, but
never sung.

III

Seeking a sign
she gazed
upon a butterfly
visiting goldenrod.

IV

Quieting her mind
she heard utterances.
Hushed vocals
once shunned, now
floated forward.

V

I love you always and in all ways.
Thank you for being in my life.
I cherish your light.

Sadness yielded
as your spirit
swaddled her.

VI

Yours are the melodies
her heart heard.
Yours are the songs
woven into her musical.

The End Game

Trying to get it all in
before the final bell

suspense building
crowd cheering

you get the ball
shoot, two points
and rebound
down the court
but the buzzer
blasts *last call*

final score:
zero to ninety-nine

Well played, Dad
Well played

Breaking Dawn

windows hissing, branches
banging against clapboard
please let the power stay on
at least until I light a candle
or find a flashlight

two hours until dawn
sleep's done when thunder
howls down the chimney
and lightning highlights the room

another hour passes
a limb cracks
sliding down the back
of the house
taking with it my power

rain spattering ceases
steel clouds cover daybreak
I pick up the phone, wanting
Con Ed's queue to be quick
and electricity restored by nightfall

Brewed Rite

nothing warmed
like a hot cup of creamed tea

a ritual learned long ago from Mom

it started with a Lipton tea bag
America's Favorite, or so
the yellow and red box declared
(generic was subpar and wouldn't do)

I took down my favored ceramic mug
unwrapped the flow thru bag, anchored its
stringed tag, poured hot water, dunked pouch
until the perfect russet brown hue emerged

removed sachet, added clotted cream

the first sip transported me back
to memories of pocket-sized pleasantries
shared around Mom's cozy kitchen table as we
drank our traditional Saturday afternoon *cuppa*

The Unseatable Bench

Avery notes:
grass screams when it is cut
tasting the blade before
being mowed down
my eyes hear your cries
for help

Meg declares:
a smell
cannot be a scream
it is but a breath
of oxygen
being released

    Welcome to the pearly gates of stupidity
    take a rest on the unseatable bench

    as Annabell tosses herself down the stairs
    screaming: *Annabell is leaving*

    the book writes itself
    because the rusty gate

    leads to hell

    her pen bleeds these words:
    the grass screams to grow
    but will be cut still
    another day

Mighty Oak: A Haibun

At the edge of the property stood the mighty oak, next to the mighty oak stood the delicate cherry blossom tree, and next to the delicate cherry blossom tree stood the all-important house. The oak grew from a tiny acorn when the land was forested. The homeowner planted the cherry tree to celebrate moving into the house. The oak provided nuts and sheltering shade. The cherry tree provided pink-budded bursts, and its sour berries fed the birds. A problem arose in the all-important house—roots disemboweled its sewer line. The plumbing was cured, but the culprit had to be found. Whose roots caused the destruction? The homeowner investigated. A chief arborist was appointed. The cherry tree pleaded roots too delicate to penetrate a plumbing pipe. The oak claimed roots too deep. The chief arborist rendered his verdict. The sentence was death. A week later, the punishment was carried out. The homeowner sealed the all-important house windows to drown out the noise.

suffer the sinewy
his tubular toughness
cut short his life

Reflection: A Golden Shovel

The Joy that isn't shared, I've heard, / dies young.
              —Anne Sexton, "Welcome Morning"

In the morning the
sun tried to shine joy
into a mirror that
sits alone. Its reflection isn't
something I want shared,

it dampened my spirit, but I've
embraced what the sun heard:
*Your shadow light dies
early. It longs to remain young.*

poem at sixty

after Sonia Sanchez, "poem at thirty"

noontime
in New York
eyes hairy
with the weight
of the world.
too tired
not to think
in cliques. no
cliché. whatever.
too tired
to care. too tired
to bother. too tired
to sleep.
once I slept
like a motherboard
waking up
freshly restored
to factory specifications.
that was before
my warranty
expired. and
the factory recall.
can they even
find the part?

This Being Human

like a vessel sailing the open seas
built structurally sound to withstand
storms, tossing and turning, and still
staying the course

using longitude and latitude
journeying to different harborages
some polarizing like the seasons
offering contrasting vistas
from tropical to glacial

exploring exotic destinations
experiencing community and multiplicity
in each sheltering anchorage

swimming

after Lucille Clifton, "climbing"

swimming upstream
against the current
the earth
guiding me
propelling me
forward
for survival
for a better life
each stroke
building strength
endurance
the effort to rebound
for sixty seasons
demands a destination
worthy of the journey

Any Other Name: A Sonnet

Practical garden rose
pleasing but no American beauty
utilitarian hardy petaled head
providing bees with pollen
creating scented breeze

Thornless rose symbolizing glorious love nearby
prickling thorn alluding to dangerous love ahead
twelve-stemmed bouquet replete with perfection
an entire year, the full zodiac, all apostles present

Holy purity of white roses
passional sacrifice of red roses
joyful wisdom of yellow roses
admiring grace of pink roses
beautiful pulchritude abounds

In the Morning

A shadow of illumination slivers
through the left corner of my blackout shades.
What the heck? It can't be morning already.

Further investigation is needed.

I tunnel out of my quilted cocoon.
My eyes unlatch, always a good thing.
Oh, yeah, morning has erupted.

I lift my head like a slow-moving crane
probing for the green digital numbers.

7:12 – not feeling that number, need to do better.

Okay, let the games begin.
What *is* an appealing time to leave
my berth and venture into the latrine?

7:17 – a balanced number, still too soon.
7:20 – a tiny round orb, but too early for philosophy.
7:25 – two plus five, math is fun, but not yet.

I finally settled on 7:30 as today's launching interval
and wait patiently for the clock to catch up.
If I miss it, there's always 7:33, I do love a double-digit.

Oscar

Filled my wine glass with ice-cold chardonnay
made a snack of cheddar cheese and crackers

placed all on the small oak table
next to my comfy club chair

stretched for my yarn satchel tucked under my feet
tried not to jar anything as I made the reach

my sweet Oscar slept soundly in my lap
while I knitted his sunflower sweater

until he let out a muffled woof, and his legs twitched
as he chased squirrels in his doggy dreams

Creating Kintsugi

Mending shattered vessel
Embracing disfigurement
Highlighting imperfections
Creating art through ruins

Gilded threads suture cracks
remedy releases artistry within

Makes it whole
bonds brokenness

Handle it now
with a gentle touch

Sacred scars strengthen
cherished container

Precious porcelain shines
with surging love

Rejoice with beauty restored
setbacks vanquished

Transforming trauma
Illuminating change
Redesigning form
I am Kintsugi

Wabi Sabi

abounding
beauty
mending
cracked cup
smoldering
scented incense
simmering
botanic tea
savoring
spicy herbs
simply
being

Fire Within

her inner Warrior kindled at birth
awakened a protective presence

flames burn within her heart, fiery hot
like heat kept on a sizzling broil

hardcore, unstoppable, unrelenting
not just surviving but thriving

facing adversity, waging battle
fighting injustice unfailingly

standing up for beliefs
speaking for those muted

persevering in the face of obstacles
and challenges, acting in the service of others

protecting those too weak
to fend for themselves

taking a stand, having a vision
modeling bravery, strength, vitality

stoking others' courageous inner fires
knowing these qualities live in all

Bluebird Sky

rinsed clean
rain refreshed

lifted my eyes
asked:

what's missing

iridescent blue ether
answered:

love daily

manifesto given
challenge accepted

illuminated sky
enheartened

Gentle Grasp

after morning rain
droplet's light is captured
like a mirrored reflection
hiding in the sun's shadow

effervescent
sighing gently
a perfect teardrop
clinging to a bud

invisible delicate hold
shimmering clean
crystal clear clarity
gasping, a delicate grasp

movement makes it tremble
relinquishing, plummeting
fading from sight
skydiving to the ground

JOY: A Golden Shovel

JOY / does not want to be / written. It does not need me.
—Seema Reza, "JOY"

Soft eyes worship warm joy
it slackens a frozen frown, that's what it does

A tree smile blossoms, how could it not
foiling complacency, striving to want
creation bursts forth—able to
end sheltering, now it is time to be

Bring forth life, or so it is written
rejuvenation abounds, there's no hiding from it

Joy thaws rigid restrictions, that's what it does
fauna flaunts fanciful buds, how can they not
after winter's weariness, springtime will need
joyful magic all around. It does not need me.

Fireflies and Marshmallows

Yesterday, okay, over half a century ago
we kid cousins lazed around all day

our bellies full of hot dogs, hamburgers
bottomless glasses of iced sweet tea

we sat around burnt coals in a metal grill
set on coltish silver legs

fireflies rose from the dusky grass
filling the yard with magical sparks

after sundown, Auntie left the card game
to find us some campfire marshmallows

we rooted out sticks as long as our arms
to pierce the sugary white puffs

watched patiently as the fire
roasted the mallows mahogany brown

we glided sticky fingers over the sweetmeat
and slid off the top grilled crusty layer

savored the charred gummy coating
then went in for the next molten bite

we touched the twigs to our tongues
to get every last *ooey gooey* morsel

not realizing we created sweet
sentiments that lazy summer day

Magic Fabric

Start with Simplicity's wrap dress pattern
classic style, comfortable to wear
flattering, easy to make
It requires three yards of plum-purple
cotton jersey fabric

Pin the cloth to   delicate tissue pattern pieces
once for the right side   once for the left
hold the pinned fabric taut on the cutting board
remove your scissors from their holster
    begin cutting on the right side
        moving toward the center
   slow and steady   measured cuts
pattern puzzle pieces begin to take form

Power up the sewing machine, thread its needle
position two pattern pieces under the feeder
apply light pressure to the foot pedal, engage needle

Gently glide the cotton jersey cloth along its journey
marrying material together, the metamorphosis begins
as fabric transforms into garment

You try on the finished product
twirling your reflection
to inspect your masterpiece

Green stockings would pair
perfectly with this purple apparel

These colors together
suit you to a tee
like a blossom on a tree

Smells Like Jersey Shore

tar coated pilings
burning sand

midway grilled sausage
vinegar crinkled fries

coconut tanning oil
boom boxes blaring

cheap henna tattoos
extra ear piercings

lifeguards whistling
riptide warnings

breezes off the bay
green flies biting

breezes off the ocean
sails billowing

boogie boards
riding waves

seagulls stealing
hamburgers grilling

salt slicks
parching lips

Canadian wildfires
streaming smoky fog

eyes burning
throat closing

woods firing
but no marshmallows roasting

Somersaults with Graceful Flips:
A Golden Shovel

> *Tell me, what is it you plan to do / With your one / wild and precious life?*
> —Mary Oliver, "The Summer Day"

How can you predict and tell
your ambitious life's work to me?

It's not so much the *what*
but the *intention* that is
profoundly important, it
(my question) asks you:
what is your lifespan action plan?

Is your heart willing to
allow your soul to do
somersaults with
graceful flips into your
spirit so you can enjoy one
vast journey along wild
spectral pathways and
inhabit this sacredly precious
adventure called life?

About the Author

Laura Daniels is a multi-genre writer and founder of the Facebook blog *The Fringe 999*. She's an active member of Women Who Write, Jersey City Writers Plum Poets, and Livingston Writers Critique Group and on Instagram @thefringe999. She holds degrees from two Jersey institutions, Rutgers University and Stevens Institute of Technology. She is a certified public accountant (CPA) and, in an earlier life, wrote continuing professional education (CPE) courses for Thomson Reuters and taught accounting at two Jersey institutions, Saint Elizabeth University (formerly College of Saint Elizabeth) and Caldwell University. Her poems grow from a love of wandering and New Jersey, where she lives with her soulmate Chris (campaignbuttons-etc.com) in Mt Arlington and works in her community garden tending her two blueberry bushes, Thelma and Louise, and visits her talented and favorite son, Jon (readingswithjon.com) in Hudson, NY.

Laura can be reached at:
lauradanielswriter.wordpress.com

www.ingramcontent.com/pod-product-compliance
Lightning Source LLC
Chambersburg PA
CBHW030915170426
43193CB00009BA/859